THE PATH

The Fathers of St. Joseph
Rule of Life

> You make known to me the path of life; you
> will fill me with joy in your presence, with
> eternal pleasures at your right hand. *Psalm* 16

THE PATH: The Fathers of St. Joseph Rule of Life

Stewardship: A Mission of Faith
11 BlackHawk Lane
Elizabethtown, PA 17022
StewardshipMission.org

Written by Devin Schadt

Cover Design: Devin Schadt

ISBN: 978-1-7327739-3-6

CONTENTS

Summoning
the Saint

Often, after a man is married and begins
having children he realizes that he needs God.
As he begins to follow Christ more intentionally,
he discovers that the Lord Jesus and the Catholic
Church summon him to be a saint—to be "all in"
for God. Though the Church has beatified men
who were fathers, compared to religious saints there
are very few; and even among those laymen who
were canonized, there exist very few who are lauded
precisely for how they embraced and lived their
fatherly vocation.

Consequently, many men succumb to the
false notion that the saint's path is reserved for
the priests, the religious, and the missionary—not
for him. He believes that his desire to be a saint is
compromised precisely because of his vocation as a
husband and father. Yet he knows he should follow
Jesus, but lacks the vision that shows how he can

become a holy man of God while living amidst the world. It is for lack of vision that my people perish (see Prov 29:18).

When a man suspects that the summons to sanctity is nearly impossible for him, he inadvertently turns to the world and its six promises: prestige, prominence, profit, pleasure, possessions, and power. The devil attempts to convince him that by obtaining these things he will be happy and fulfilled. But if he decides to be allured by these worldly dreams, he will encounter three obstacles: God, his wife, and his children. Most men compromise and believe that they can have their fair share of the six promises while appearing to be a Christian man. He pursues the world, while doing the minimum to maintain his family. He wagers that he can have the world and still have heaven.

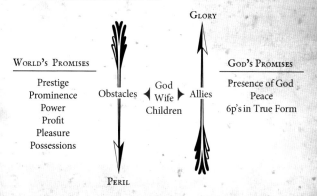

GLORY

WORLD'S PROMISES

Prestige
Prominence
Power
Profit
Pleasure
Possessions

Obstacles ◀ God Wife Children ▶ Allies

GOD'S PROMISES

Presence of God
Peace
6p's in True Form

PERIL

What if there is another way? What if there exists a path to sanctity that has been veiled, virtually unnoticed, seldom proclaimed? What if your wife and children are not obstacles, but a way to the Way? What if your vocation as head of your family is your path to be a saint?

By becoming a protector, provider, and priest, a father obtains the presence of God, and therefore will be afforded true pleasure and peace. His vocation is the path to sainthood; and if he lives it, he acquires true prestige, true prominence, true power, true profit, the right kind of pleasure, and is afforded a peace beyond all understanding. He bestows upon his kin the legacy of sanctity.

This booklet is an attempt to afford every man the opportunity to understand, embrace, live, and share the way of fatherly greatness, founded upon St. Joseph, who was husband, father, and head of his family.

THIS LITTLE BOOKLET BRIEFLY OUTLINES:

1. *The purpose* of a Father of St. Joseph

2. *The path* to be a man of glory while living amidst the world and the family

3. *The 4 pillars* upon which a man will establish a life of glory

4. *The 7 principles* of a spiritual leader's rule of life

5. *The 33 practices* that help him apply St. Joseph's way of life in our modern world in a practical way

The FOSJ rule of life can be summarized as:
1 Path | 4 Pillars | 7 Principles | 33 Practices
The foundation of a man's success is his rule of life.

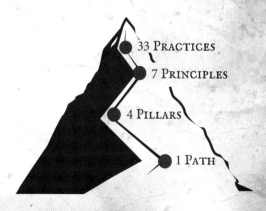

33 PRACTICES
7 PRINCIPLES
4 PILLARS
1 PATH

St. Joseph's Way of Life

The Fathers of St. Joseph offers a way of life for men and fathers that spans all ages. A program is temporary; a way of life is enduring, timeless, and sanctifying. Just as the Dominicans, Benedictines, Franciscans, and Carmelites all have a particular rule of life, so also the human father has a pattern for holiness that is founded upon the life and spirituality of St. Joseph.

Today's father needs to know that he too has a specific vocation, a rule of life that if followed will aid him in becoming a man of glory. And just as each of those spiritualities played a major part in building the Church and claiming souls for Christ, we pray that St. Joseph's way of life will also play its part in the conversion of the nations.

Welcome to the worldwide movement of the Fathers of St. Joseph, whose aim is nothing less than the redemption, revitalization, and restoration of fatherhood. We believe that society goes by way of the family, and the family goes by way of the father. If we want to change the world, we fathers must change.

The
Purpose

The purpose of the Fathers of St. Joseph's rule of life is fourfold:

1 *He embodies the three characteristics of a FOSJ: Humble, Silent, Hidden*

A Father of St. Joseph spends his energies donating himself to the cause of leading his wife and children to the glory of God, by establishing his vocation upon St. Joseph's four pillars (see pp 18-19). By doing so, he embodies the characteristics of a FOSJ: humble, silent, and hidden.

② *He prays for the restoration, redemption, and revitalization of fatherhood*

A Father of St. Joseph, while living amidst the world, offers his daily work—in union with his prayers and sacrifices—to God for the restoration, redemption, and revitalization of fatherhood. He believes that the conversion of the world is dependent upon the renewal of the Church; that the renewal of the Church is dependent upon the restoration and revitalization of marriages and families; and that this renewal of all things is dependent upon the head of the family.

FOSJ Four Purposes

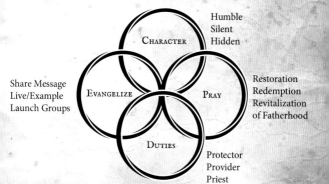

Humble
Silent
Hidden

Share Message
Live/Example
Launch Groups

Restoration
Redemption
Revitalization
of Fatherhood

Protector
Provider
Priest

3 *He embraces the three duties of a FOSJ: Protector, Provider, and Priest*

If a man is a servant while neglecting being a leader, he becomes a doormat. If a man is a leader while neglecting to be a servant, he becomes a tyrant. To be like St. Joseph "lord of his house" (see Ps 105:21) a father leads by serving as a protector, provider, and priest of his domestic church.

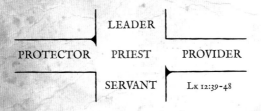

4 *He executes the three FOSJ evangelization goals: Share the Message, Live by Example, and Establish Groups*

A man who experiences the effects of The Fathers of St. Joseph's rule of life responds to Christ's great commission to evangelize the nations. He accomplishes this by sharing the spirituality with other men; being an exemplary witness as one who has built his life upon St. Joseph's four pillars; and he establishes fraternal groups with the purpose of forming men in St. Joseph's rule of life.

The Path

Your identity leads to your destiny. A man can only discover who he is by giving himself away. Your vocation as a father-leader is the context in which you are to continually give yourself away and discover who you are, your mission, and your destiny. Your identity is discovered by means of living your vocation, which leads to your destiny, which is to be a saint who glorifies God and is glorified by God. God wants to glorify you (see 2 Thes 2:14).

Your fatherly vocation as head of your family is your path to sanctification and leading your family to God. This is the path. If you are a husband and father no other path will be given. To remain on this path is one of the greatest challenges posed to a man. To validate this point, we can consider the vast amount of divorces, broken families, and children

Your Destiny
(God's Glory in You)

The Path: Your Vocation

Your Identity
(Discovered on the Path)

growing up in single-parent households without their father. There is a mountain of statistical data and research that demonstrates that the absence of the male spiritual leader causes familial and societal breakdown.

The evil one's intent is to remove you from this path. To remain steadfast on this path and to fulfill your vocational mission is the singular goal of the father-saint. This is your biggest battle.

The Pillars

To remain steadfast on the path to holiness and resist the ever-pressing temptations to flee from his vocation, a Father of St. Joseph builds his life upon the four pillars of St. Joseph's spirituality: embrace silence, embrace woman, embrace the child, embrace charitable authority. St. Joseph consistently embraced the silence to discern God's will. This silence led to the action of embracing the Blessed Virgin Mary and the child Jesus. Joseph embraced his God-given authority as head of the Holy family and became a superhuman oblation for the purpose of Jesus and Mary fulfilling the holy will of God.

By embracing silence, we learn to pray like St. Joseph. Such prayer is the foundation of trust that is at the heart of being a disciple of Jesus Christ and a trusting son of God. By embracing woman, a Father of St. Joseph strives to overcome lust in all its forms, bears his wife's burdens as his own, and loves her as Christ loves the Church. By embracing the child, a Father of St. Joseph becomes the face, the voice, and the touch of the Father that his child cannot see, hear, or feel. By embracing charitable authority, a Father of St. Joseph becomes a protector, provider, and priest of his domestic church.

The "just man," St. Joseph faithfully built his spiritual house upon these four pillars and is aptly named "Pillar of Families." A man becomes the pillar of his own family when he builds his vocation upon these four pillars.

Four Pillars of St. Joseph

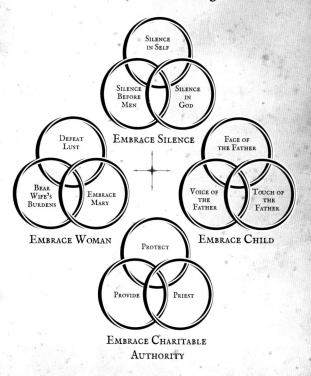

The Purpose
of the Practices

Though a man may make spiritual practices, spiritual practices do not make the man. Though a man may attempt to use spirituality to transform himself into a saint, it is God who uses spirituality to transform a man into a saint. To be clear, neither a spiritual plan of life, nor a man, can make a man a saint. Only God can make the man into a saint. If we begin to believe that by performing, and even successfully completing our spiritual practices, we are climbing the mountain of glory ourselves—by our own doing—we are certain to fall from the precipice as a result of pride.

The call to sanctity can consist of active sacrifices and passive sufferings.

If the spiritual journey of a man is to be likened to that of a gardener, then active sacrifices can be compared to the toil and labor demanded of the gardener to prepare the soil. Indeed, this is his primary duty: to prepare the soil by means of his active sacrifices—those he has personally chosen for himself. Such active sacrifices are not the seed, nor the water, nor the sun, or that which makes the seed grow. His active sacrifices till and open the soil to receive the seed; then after the seed is planted, his active sacrifices continue to serve as fertilizer that aids the plant's growth. Nevertheless, all such labor should be understood as nothing more than fertilizer.

The fundamental difference between active and passive sacrifices is that active sacrifices are those we choose for ourselves. We determine whether we take on sufferings and mortifications. We determine the intensity, the duration, the type, and the level of the mortification; and when it moves even a hair beyond what we believe we can handle, we discontinue the sacrifice or lessen the intensity of it. In other words, active sacrifices are completely under our control.

Passive sufferings and sacrifices are those God chooses for us. He determines their intensity, type, level, and duration. We have very little—if any—

control over them. Indeed, this lack of control, and lack of knowledge as to when the suffering will cease, and what areas of our life it will affect, only intensify the suffering. It is necessary that the passive suffering becomes an active sacrifice by offering it to the Lord Jesus, lest it remain only a suffering.

Between these two sacrifices is a vast gulf, likened to the difference between a man's works, which are like filthy rags (see Isaiah 64:6), and God's action in the soul, which is like Christ transforming water into wine (see Jn 2). In fact, our sacrifices are like the water, and passive sufferings, if embraced, are like Christ's act of transforming the water into wine. Both are needed; yet only God can provide the transformation.

Considering this, The Fathers of St. Joseph spiritual practices are not to be misunderstood as a checklist that will make one holy. In fact, our journey will demand that we exercise greater faith in what God is doing in us, and less reliance on our own doing. Our prayers and practices are a way to till the hardened soil of our hearts. By means of this cultivation, the soil of our hearts is better prepared to receive the seed of the Holy Spirit, which alone can transform us and give us a heart devoted to God.

What God Does

PASSIVE SUFFERINGS — God Transforms the Soul

ACTIVE SACRIFICES — Prepares the Soul for God

What We Do

Motives
Matter

The underlying "why" behind what we do is often more important than the outcome of what we do. Someone may be well known because of his apparent charity; yet if his motive behind such acts of charity is to use charity as a means to become lauded, then it is not charity per se, but vanity. Similarly, one can use prayer, fasting, and almsgiving—all good in themselves—to glorify oneself rather than to glorify God. If a man glorifies God, God cannot help but glorify a man; but he ought to let God determine how he is glorified.

The motivation behind the FOSJ spiritual practices is not as much about us as it is about God and others. The man who fasts for others may consequently have the added benefit of losing weight; yet his primary motive was not to lose weight but to "gain" grace for others. If the motive behind these daily practices is for love of God and love of neighbor, the participant will also benefit greatly from these practices, for God will not be outdone in generosity.

THE MOTIVATION BEHIND THESE PRACTICES IS FOURFOLD:

> *First, to repent and do penance for our sins;*
>
> *Second, as an act of thanksgiving for Christ's sacrifice of Himself for our sins and His redemptive work in us;*
>
> *Third, as a priestly sacrifice for the spiritual and temporal well-being and salvation of others; and*
>
> *Lastly, to grow in love of and communion with God and with those entrusted to our fatherly care.*

A Father of St. Joseph offers his daily practices as an act of penance for those times in which he has neglected his vocational responsibility; as an act of thanksgiving to God for his marriage and family; as an offering for the salvation and sanctification of his wife and children; and lastly, for a more profound personal communion with God.

These practices are not to be viewed as an arbitrary imposition, but rather as an outgrowth of the four pillars that constitute St. Joseph's way of life. Though these practices should not be perceived as a harsh rule, nevertheless one ought to strive to complete them to the best of one's ability and state of life. By doing so, one's life will be built upon the four pillars of St. Joseph. Though it may appear that God asks much of you, be not dismayed or disheartened, the spiritual benefits that God grants to a man who lives this rule of life are numerous, effective, and transformative. God is calling you to be a saint; and your vocation is the path by which you are to climb this mountain.

The Seven
Principles

The Fathers of St. Joseph rule of life is founded upon seven practical principles that, if lived, will help prepare a man for real transformation. Spiritual practices that are associated with each of the seven principles are listed below the particular principle. A man can, over time, prayerfully and consistently build his own rule of life by applying the spiritual practices that are appropriate for his state in life.

One suggested way to accomplish this is by incorporating one or two spiritual principles into your life per week. For example, at the beginning of Week One, a man applies the first FOSJ principle "Commit to Daily Prayer Practices," by selecting a practice(s) from the list beneath the principle and beginning the practice. (See p. 30 for the list and description of each of the Spiritual Practices.)

The key is to select one or two practices and focus on doing them well and doing them consistently. The seven weeks (forty-nine days) of incorporating the spiritual principles and practices can be likened to preparing for Day 50, a new Pentecost, in hope that God's Holy Spirit will operate more fully in a man's life.

THE SEVEN PRINCIPLES:

1. *Commit to Daily Prayer Practices*
   Practices 1-7

2. *Commit to Secret Sacrifice*
   Practices 8-11

3. *Commit to Embracing Your Wife*
   Practices 12-17

4. *Commit to Building the Domestic Church*
   Practices 18-22

5. *Commit to Embracing Your Child*
   Practices 23-26

6. *Commit to Living the Liturgical Life*
   Practices 27-30

7. *Commit to Working for God*
   Practices 31-33

The 33
Practices

1. DAILY MORNING OFFERING

Upon waking, prior to viewing any emails or texts—
or doing anything else—drop down to the floor
and surrender yourself and your day, to God. By
previewing or viewing texts or emails, listening to
podcasts, music, or the news, prior to your morning
offering, you will have surrendered to the world
instead of giving your first fruits to God. In addition,
when possible make your morning offering on your
knees and with your head bowed down to the floor.
The reason for this is that your body expresses
what your soul believes. By kneeling or praying in
a prostrate position, you bodily express that you
are spiritually submitting and surrendering your
soul to God's Holy Will. Your morning offering
consists of offering to God the Father all that you
are and have, through, with, and in His Son, Jesus

Christ; imploring the Holy Spirit to animate and direct you throughout the day; offering yourself to Jesus Christ in the manner by which He came to us: through the union of the Virgin Mary and St. Joseph. The purpose behind your morning offering is simply "reporting for duty," acknowledging to God your worship of Him, and your readiness to serve Him wholeheartedly.

Sample morning offering: Heavenly Father, I offer you my day; all that I am and have to you—spiritual, temporal, physical, my thoughts, memory, will, and good actions—through, with, and in your Son, our Lord, Jesus Christ, in union with all the Masses offered throughout the world, for the conversion of sinners, for the reparation of sins, for the holy souls in purgatory to be drawn into your Divine Light, and most of all, for the love of Thee, My God. Lord Jesus, I do not presume to come to you alone; but rather approach you in the way You came to us, through the holy union of the Blessed Virgin and St. Joseph, her chaste spouse. Holy Mary, good St. Joseph, by your union of wills and your intercession before God, obtain for me the gift of the Holy Spirit, that our Lord Jesus may be conceived ever anew and ever more fully in me. My guardian angel intercede for me.

2. Daily Litany of St. Joseph

The litany of St. Joseph is one way to quickly offer St. Joseph honor, while also becoming acquainted with his gifts and virtues, which we ought to imitate. * See the Litany of St. Joseph on p.76

3. Daily Examination of Conscience

Toward the end of day, prior to retiring for the evening or before getting into bed, take a couple of moments to examine your conscience. To do this, assume a prayerful position such as kneeling or lying prostrate, and invoke the Holy Spirit to help you examine your thoughts, words, and actions made throughout the day. This does not need to be an exacting process. Ideally, first recount the blessings of the day and give God thanks for them. Second, reflect upon and confess to God your actions, thoughts, and words that were not in conformity with God's Holy Will or are sinful. Third, after confessing your sins, make a heartfelt act of contrition, asking God for His mercy, forgiveness, and the grace necessary to avoid the near occasion of sin in the future. The Ten Commandments can be used as a guide by which one can examine his conscience, but sometimes these commandments may be too broad and general. Another powerful way to examine yourself is by using Christ's Beatitudes:

Blessed are the poor in Spirit . . . Was I prideful, self-seeking, self-glorifying, self-important, placing myself above others today? Have I responded to the people and circumstances in my life with humility, accepting them as though they are from God?

Blessed are the meek . . . Did I allow anger to be the driving force behind my actions? Did I vent my anger, raise my voice, and act in a demeaning way toward those around me? Do I allow Church politics, government politics, family situations, obstacles at work or at home to arouse my anger?
Or do I give such situations to God and allow the Holy Spirit to help me deal with them rationally and calmly?

Blessed are those who mourn . . . Do I have true sorrow and contrition for my sins? Have I repented and done penance for my past sins? Do I seriously consider that my sins of the past may have led individuals to sin against God, perhaps even damnation? Do I ask God to make right my wrongs, and redeem my omissions? Do I consider that it was for my sins that the Son of God was tortured and gave His life?

Blessed are those who hunger and thirst for righteousness ...
Do I desire the right over the wrong, the moral over
the immoral? Do I rejoice when evil or immorality
is lauded? Do I approve of videos, movies, posts, and
tweets that contain illicit or immoral messages? Do
I share such things, or find humor in them? Am I fair
in my dealings with others, particularly in business and
finances? Have I stolen anyone's goods, content, or
good reputation? If so, have I made amends? Justice
is seeking God first and giving Him His due: Do I
seek God first in all matters? Do I give God the first
fruits of my money and time?

Blessed are the merciful ... Have I withheld forgiving
someone who has offended me? Have I sought
forgiveness from someone I have offended or sinned
against? Have I judged, condemned, or criticized
another unjustly? Have I judged another without
considering my own wretchedness, failings, and sins?

Blessed are the pure of heart ... Do I view the
human body as an object of desire, to be used for
my disordered gratification? Do I use pornography
in any form? Do I avoid or do I submit to the temptation
to click on ads, posts, or news feeds that display
people in sexually provocative situations? Do I
make every attempt to see a woman as an equal,
with equal dignity, or do I reduce her to her bodily
attributes? Do I use or manipulate people to obtain

what I desire from them? Or do I love my neighbor for whom they are, without expecting anything in return? Have I been jealous or envious of another, another's status, talents, gifts, or possessions? Do I praise God for His glory in others, even when I don't possess that particular glory?

Blessed are those who suffer persecution for justice and Christ's sake . . . Am I ashamed to share or display my belief in Jesus Christ? Am I afraid to pray in public? Do I avoid discussing my faith with others? Do I avoid or neglect protecting another's good actions, just cause, or beliefs in God because I am afraid of being persecuted?

4. Pray for Each Member of Your Family

This practice should go unsaid. As the priest of your family, it is your responsibility to present your wife and children, their intentions, needs, and spiritual and physical well-being to God daily. This indicates that you need to be aware of what is happening in their lives and know what their needs are. Your greatest petition for your wife and children, beyond worldly success, achievements, accomplishments, or acceptance by others, is their salvation and sanctification. Therefore, as the chief representative of your family, you are asking God to lavishly bless and grant favor to each member of your family.

5. Daily Morning Prayer
(15 minutes/including 5 minutes of silence)

Secularists have been known to say, "Win the morning, win the day." The truth of this idea is born from the Christian ideal, particularly the monastic life, wherein the man who seeks God first is blessed in his work, efforts, and initiatives. Indeed, the Christian who gives God his morning's first moments will be given God's presence throughout his day. There exist many methods and forms of prayer that are far too numerous to mention here. The main purpose of your morning prayer is to allow yourself the time and space to cultivate a relationship with God and be drawn into His Trinitarian communion of Persons. Morning prayer is different than the morning offering in that the morning offering is reporting for duty and asking God's blessing on one's day; whereas the purpose of morning prayer is to be with and to rest with God. Morning prayer consists of worship and praise, divine revelation as the source of conversation with God, and offering petitions. To cultivate this divine conversation, a primer is very helpful, such as the Liturgy of the Hours, Sacred Scripture, or a reflection from a reliable devotional. The Liturgy of the Hours is an excellent resource that helps one "converse" with God by using preset Psalms, prayers, and petitions that are segmented by the time, or "hours," of the day.

"Lauds" is the morning prayer of the Church. Regardless of what source you use as the "launching pad" for your prayer with God, we must remember that these things are not "prayer" itself, but the "gas" that is poured on the hot coals of God's presence within the soul. The Holy Spirit then fans these embers into flame. After you have conversed with God, spend several minutes in silence, waiting upon Him. This time is essential to allowing God the time and space to speak or infuse Himself into your soul. After this period of silence, offer your petitions and thanksgiving to him; and if possible, make a resolution that you will carry out throughout your day. End your prayer with a Glory Be.

6. Daily Rosary

The Rosary is the chain that binds Satan. The Rosary is not a mere repetition of idle words. It is a devotion to Our Blessed Mother, who leads us in meditation on Christ's life. Indeed, by "holding her hand," we see Jesus and His life through her eyes; and feeling with her heart, she helps to unlock the sacred mysteries of Christ's life, from his Incarnation through His Ascension, and the outpouring of His Holy Spirit on the Church. There exists a grave temptation or at least a tendency to rush through the prayers of the Rosary, rattling them off like an auctioneer; or to zone out and think of other things while saying the words. Due to the repetitive nature of the prayer, it is easy to understand how these things happen. To overcome such temptations, it is important to remember that the quality of prayer is more important than the quantity of words. The Rosary is a journey with Mary, following Christ and learning to be His disciple. Considering this it can be highly beneficial to begin praying the Rosary by praying only one or two decades or by using a scriptural Rosary. A scriptural Rosary allows one to enter more deeply into the mystery being meditated upon by reciting a brief scriptural passage for each bead prior to praying the Hail Mary. For example, if you are praying the First Sorrowful Mystery, before saying the first Hail Mary, recite the Scripture: "Jesus took His disciples to the garden of Gethsemane and asked them to watch and pray." Prior to the second Hail Mary, you may recite the next chronological passage, "Jesus said to His disciples, 'Pray that you may not fall into temptation.'" Prior to the third Hail Mary, "For the spirit is willing, but the flesh is weak," and so on. By praying the Rosary this way, you will be able to penetrate more deeply into the sacred mysteries of Christ, and thus His prayer can become very meaningful and profitable.

7. Evening Prayer

It has been said that how we finish our day is how we will finish our life. If we finish our day faithful in prayer and devotion, most likely we will complete our days devoted, faithful, and in prayer. The purpose of evening prayer is to offer worship to God and to cultivate conversation with God. As with morning prayer, to assist in fostering this conversation, a primer such as the Liturgy of Hours, Sacred Scripture, or a reflection from a reliable devotional is very helpful. The Liturgy of the Hours helps one converse with God, by using preset Psalms, prayers and petitions that are segmented by the time, or "hours," of the day: Vespers is the evening prayer of the Church. Prior to beginning evening prayer, spend a couple of moments in the presence of God, thanking Him for the blessings of the day and examining your conscience. After your examination of conscience, spend some time with God using Sacred Scripture, the Liturgy of the Hours, or a reflection. After you have conversed with God, spend several minutes in silence, waiting upon Him. This time is essential to allowing God the time and space to speak or infuse Himself into your soul. An important note: we are often tempted to wind down by spending time on social media prior to sleep. Without realizing it, we are giving Satan a foothold in our spiritual life. After your evening prayer, avoid all social media and surrender your sleep to God.

8. One Daily Hidden Significant Sacrifice

It has been said that prayer without sacrifice is lip service, and sacrifice without prayer is a form of bodily training and self-mastery. Prayer inspires one to sacrifice; and sacrifice inspires the power of prayer. As priest of your domestic church, it is vital that you not only pray, but also sacrifice for your family's sanctity daily. If your sacrifice is to be efficacious, that is, able to transmit grace, it must have the character of secrecy, of being hidden. "Do not let your right hand know what your left hand is doing..." (Mt 6:3). The Pharisees were said to blow a horn as they made a monetary donation, and Christ, speaking of them, said that they received their reward. Our sacrifice, therefore, is to be hidden; you are to perform the action without discussing or bringing attention to it; for by drawing attention to yourself, you have negated the power of the offering. A man who sacrifices does so in the image and imitation of the Heavenly Father who "is in secret" (Mt 6:6). If our fatherhood is to reflect and reveal the fatherhood of God, we are to carry out our sacrifices in a hidden way. Be not worried or concerned that you will not be rewarded. Glorify yourself and you will receive that reward. Glorify God and He cannot help but to glorify you; and this glory far surpasses any glory we can give ourselves. In addition to the sacrifice being secret, it ought to be significant;

that is, your offering should cost you something. By setting aside that which you desire, are attached to, or have come to depend upon, and giving it to God as an offering, it becomes "holy," set apart, that God may use it to confer grace on you, your family, and humanity in the manner He sees fit. Suggested sacrifices that have the character of significance for the average man are: sleeping on the floor; not using a pillow while you sleep; rising an hour early for prayer; committing to waking when the alarm rings without delay; taking a cold shower; skipping a meal(s); drinking nothing other than water; abstaining from alcohol; abstaining from sexual relations with your wife for a period of time; abstaining from the use of social media; donating money that you want to use for your own desires to a good cause; adoring the Blessed Sacrament several times a week, etc. The key is that the sacrifice be daily; that the motive is for God and the conversion of your family, Christian brothers, neighbors, and their families; that it is accomplished with the motivation of love and not necessarily "self-help" (for example: to lose weight); and that the sacrifice be hidden, as much as possible.

9. REDUCE FORMS OF MEDIA SUCH AS RADIO, MUSIC, INTERNET, NEWS, VIDEOS

To become capable of discerning the still, small, interior voice of God, it is vital that the voices of the world be muted. Without this first step, it will be gravely difficult to discern God's mission, vision, and plan for your life. A first step to becoming a man of silence who is capable of receiving God's impulses and divine inspirations is to silence the radio, music, news, and social media feeds while driving in the car or commuting. By doing so, your drive time can become prayer time—a very natural form of meditating—wherein you invite God into the areas of your life where you need divine guidance. Though at first it may feel awkward to be in silence, eventually your soul will crave such moments of solitude and eventually you will begin to notice that God is shaping your conscience and your motivations. Indeed, you will notice the effect of God's presence in your life.

10. Avoid Grumbling/Complaining About or Demeaning Family Members

Complaining and grumbling about your children, your occupation, coworkers, friends, neighbors, finances, your house, politics, the Church, and especially yourself, is a toxic poison that will not only make you appear weak, but will also place a massive burden on your wife. A good wife will often desire to fix things her husband struggles with, only to discover that she cannot. When this occurs, she begins to embody the stress, which can manifest itself in very negative ways, such as ill health, mental and psychological stress, depression and anxiety, or a lack of desire to thrive and live. As protector of your family, it is your duty to protect your wife first and foremost from yourself. To do this, every time you are tempted to complain, rather than doing so, find something encouraging and hopeful to focus on. If there is something that needs to be discussed that is problematic or needs resolving, commit yourself not to complain about the situation; but rather, consider ways that the situation can be redeemed. Additionally, one of the most damaging things a man can do to himself and his marriage is to consistently speak negatively about himself. Your wife wants a leader, a lover, a spiritual warrior who is full of encouragement, hope, and confidence. If she senses that her husband has lost hope in himself, she may feel she is the reason for his personal sense of failure. In addition to this, she may even begin to look for the "confident warrior" in other men. "This is God's will for you: In all circumstances give thanks to God" (1 Thes 5:16). By being thankful to God for the good and the bad, the sufferings and the joys, you will become a man of confidence and joy; and such joy is contagious—especially in your marriage and family. Additionally, and perhaps more importantly, refrain from demeaning your wife in front of your children. Your show of disrespect to your wife will grant your children permission to disrespect their mother. Speaking critically of your wife or children has lasting, negative consequences that can take a lifetime to overcome. Words have a way of enduring in the person's heart long after they have been uttered.

11. Tithe Regularly/Give to the Poor

One the most effective ways that a child learns to be generous is witnessing their father giving generously to those in need. Sometimes, a dad will give his child the money to put in the collection basket at Mass; or have his child give money to the homeless person; or food to a homeless person involve his child in this act of generosity. This almost always grants divine consolation and instills a love for the less fortunate. A generous father teaches his child that God the Father is generous. Indeed, if you as a human father help the poor, your child, who perhaps feels poor in spirit, will trust that God is generous and will provide. To be intentional in this area, keep extra cash on hand, so that if the occasion in which you are asked for help arises, you can provide. Archbishop Fulton Sheen, when asked, after giving money to beggars, why he did so when he knew they would probably misuse the money, responded, "Because I do not know which one is Jesus." A child will see Christ in his father who sees Christ in the poor.

12. Weekly/Biweekly Date with your Wife

The greatest gift that a man, a father, can impart to his children is a united, harmonious, loving marriage with his wife. Security breeds security; love begets love. When children see the visible example of two people striving toward union in God, they become secure, confident, and cannot help but want to experience and replicate such love. Too often, particularly as the family grows, life's responsibilities and obligations become complicated and overwhelming. Often, without noticing, years pass before a married couple realizes that they have grown distant from one another, and in growing distant, they have grown cold in their love for one another. By making a weekly/biweekly date a priority, you will give your wife the opportunity to know that she is the most important person in your life, while also sending this message to your children. Your date with your wife does not need to be expensive, or a dinner out, but it can be that. The vital characteristics of a date are: that you have private time that extends for a couple of hours; that your wife is listened to—not judged; that you look into her eyes and discover the woman you married and that you help her feel this affection; and that you tell her she is beautiful and that you love her. A woman often forgets that she is beautiful because her husband has forgotten her beauty. To be affirmed in her beauty is one of her fundamental needs. By means of consistent dating, you will begin to see her beauty anew. Some couples will go out to a restaurant weekly, which can become costly; yet it will be the best money they will ever spend. Other couples have their date night at home, in a private area of the house away from the children, though this can be distracting. Regardless, the main point is that your weekly/biweekly date with your wife reminds her that she is a priority in your life and she is loved. Another important point is that even if you and your wife are having a difficult time, or are in the midst of conflict, it is important, if possible, not to avoid the weekly date. In fact, often by sitting across the table from one another, looking into each other's eyes, the disagreement diminishes or is resolved. Prudence is demanded, but if the couple is sincere in their desire for a better marriage, a date will help.

13. One Daily Intentional Act of Encouragement /Affection to Your Wife

St. John of the Cross said, "Where there is no love, put love, and there will be love." Often, a man can believe that because he is not "getting" what he wants from his marriage, that he has the right to distance himself from his wife. Yet, if you were to intentionally express your affection and encouragement to your wife daily, you would be putting love where perhaps there is no love, and eventually there will be love. Often, after birthing children, hormonal shifts, the loss of muscle mass, a woman can gain weight, and over time the effects of age and time catch up. This is a cause to reaffirm her continually in her beauty and express that you delight in her—because she is fearful that you don't delight in her. Actions such as simply telling her that you are thankful she is your wife, or that she is beautiful; giving her a kiss and telling her you love her; mentioning that her new hair style looks good, or that you like the way she looks in what she is wearing; that she is a dedicated mother and wife, and without her your life would be miserable—these are a small sampling of ways to express your admiration and affection to her. Often, a man can become embittered or resentful because his wife is not interested in sexual intercourse with him or has distanced herself from him in this area. If this resentment is not addressed, and if it takes hold of him, it may be a matter of time before he falls prey to sexual sins and his marriage is undermined, if not destroyed. Though it may be counterintuitive, rather than shunning your wife because of her lack of attention to your sexual needs, you ought to reinvest yourself in her by means of acts of encouragement and affection—not for what you will get out of it, but for what you can put into it. If this is done in a self-giving manner, your wife more often than not may desire to give herself in return to you. Regardless, this is a sure path to becoming a saint: to love your wife and express it, especially when you don't "feel like it." Keep in mind Jesus Christ, who embraced the Cross for His bride—despite His flesh not "feeling like it."

14. BE FAITHFUL TO YOUR WEDDING VOWS

This needs no explanation. On the day of your wedding you vowed to be faithful to your wife until death. This commitment is a living figure and symbol of Christ's fidelity to His Church. Your mission is to be a living witness and expression of this faithful, undying love—no matter what comes. Lust in all its forms is the devil's weapon to separate love from sacrifice. Pornography is not the ultimate enemy. Satan is. He uses pornography as a weapon to bind the strong man and paralyze him from leading his family effectively. For how can he teach about and lead his family to Christ if he is bound by sin? He cannot. The devil's aim is to incapacitate you; and lust, pornography, and affairs are several of his methods to accomplish this. It is important to realize that the sins you commit are in a mysterious way transferred to your children. If lust and the use of pornography, or an adulterous relationship, have become addictive pattern in your life, it is imperative that you go to confession weekly, if not twice a week; see a professional psychologist (if necessary); develop friendships to hold you accountable in this area; and increase your prayer time. Faithfulness is the proof of love; and faithfulness demands sacrifice of our disordered attachments.

15. Pray with Your Wife Once a Day

Though a husband may pray with his wife during times of family prayer, it is important that he and his wife have a short, personal, prayer time, wherein they pray specifically for God to bless and heal their marriage, and bless and sanctify their children. These private, personal prayer times between couples unite the heart of the two into one and bless the marriage in unquantifiable ways. As protector of your domestic church, the enemy is more easily overcome by means of a harmonious, united marriage than by a father or mother who has their own individual faith.

16. Bless Your Wife Daily

As priest of your domestic church, God has entrusted you with the noble duty of conferring His blessing upon those in your care, which includes your wife. Though this may initially feel awkward, simply trace the cross over her forehead, and say, "May the Father, Son, and Holy Spirit bless you now and forever." As you begin to feel more comfortable with this practice, you may add special intentions, and ask

God for particular graces and favors for your wife. This practice can concur with your private prayer time with your wife, ending your brief time of prayer by blessing her. Initially, this demands great courage to overcome the feeling of vulnerability and rejection. The feeling of awkwardness is an indication that the evil one hates this devotion and wants you to neglect your duty. Indeed, by blessing your wife God will provide many graces that unify your marriage.

17. 10 Minutes of Daily Intentional Time with Your Wife

Family life is often busy, chaotic, and overwhelming. A mother can be swept away in the emotional and temporal demands of caring for her children. She needs time to share with her husband how she is interpreting her children's welfare and her own motherhood, along with her personal existence as a human being. In other words, she needs time to share her heart. Communication leads to communion. If a husband wants true, authentic, deep communion with his wife, he will need to set aside a little time each day to hear his wife's heart. This daily communication leads to the couple being comfortable with expressing their personal needs to one another. This ability to feel secure and safe in expressing needs is essential to a healthy marriage. It is important to always bear in mind that no spouse can fulfill their spouse's needs—only Christ can. Yet, what makes a spouse feel, experience, and know that he or she is loved is when the spouse intentionally attempts to address the other's need. However, a husband cannot address his wife's needs if she is not communicating them to him—and vice versa. For this reason, ten minutes of daily intentional time with your wife will help the two of you become expert communicators and experience true communion in Christ.

18. Nightly Family Dinner

There appears to be a direct correlation between the massive decrease in families eating dinner together and the decline in Mass attendance. The family dinner reflects Holy Mass. As father of your family, you are like the Heavenly Father, who gathers His family around the "altar"—that is, your dinner table. Prior to dinner, gather the family around the goods that God has given, and together offer Him thanksgiving from your heart. As priest of your family, you not only lead your family in this ode of gratitude, but also instill this virtue of thanksgiving in each of your family members. Family dinner is the "safe zone." This is not the place to discipline your children for not completing their chores, or for failing in math. Family dinner is a time in which you can help foster joyful, encouraging conversation about important topics by asking each family member: How was your day? What made it good/bad? Tell me a little more about this... It is good to tell stories from your past or recent experiences that relate to a topic, making your time enjoyable but also educational. As a father you are to help your children understand and interpret the world and current events in light of the Gospel. The main point is that your family becomes bonded to God through your gratitude, and also bonded to you through healthy conversations. You are an icon of God the Father. If you express interest in each of your family member's lives, they will more likely believe that they are interesting and worthy of interest, and that God is interested in them. One major obstacle to family dinner in the modern age is the overwhelming amount of extracurricular activities and commitments. Evaluate whether these activities are at the service of your family, or whether your family is at the service of these activities. Determine which activities are a priority and sacrifice the others. Often, we sacrifice the family for the sake of activities, rather than sacrificing activities for the sake of God and the family. If nightly family dinner is impossible, make every effort to identify at least three nights a week that your family will meet for dinner. Good food, good conversation, prayer with thanksgiving, and an interested father's heart are the key elements to your family dinner.

19. Sacred Images

Mindfulness of responsibilities and the commitment to duty often can become a cause for inadvertently forgetting about God, His Son, Jesus, and the saints who are cheering us on to victory (see Heb 12:4). God is a family, a trinity of Persons, and has created the human race to be an eternal part of this family. The saints are those who are fully embraced as family members of God's house. We hang photos of family members to remind us of them. How much more do we benefit by having sacred images of Jesus Christ, the Sacred Heart, a crucifix, the Blessed Mother, St. Joseph, or a scene from the Gospel hanging on the walls of our home? These sacred images offer us a continual reminder to call upon our family in heaven to aid us as we travail this valley of tears. Additionally, these images leave an imprint of the divine upon our children's souls, reminding them to raise their hearts and minds to those things above and not the things below (see Col 3).

20. Sunday Gospel Reflection

The Word of God is powerful, capable of discerning thoughts and transforming the human heart (see Heb 12:4). Often, when we hear the Gospel on Sunday, we overlook or miss powerful lessons contained in the Word. Even though a priest gives a homily that expounds on the Gospel, the message may not resonate in our children's hearts. A way to prepare our children to receive more from the Gospel is by selecting a weeknight to read the upcoming Sunday's Gospel during family prayer time and discuss it. Themes and ideas that arise from your discussion will help your child to understand the Gospel more clearly, so that at Mass, your child will benefit more from the proclamation of the Word. Some ways to make Sunday Gospel reflection beneficial are:

1) Select a particular night of the week to have your Sunday Gospel reflection and keep it consistent.

2) Read it ahead of time and consider what you think the Lord may be communicating to you.

3) Have one of your family members read the Gospel.

4) After the reading the Gospel, say together, "Praise to you Lord Jesus Christ." 5) After the reading, ask your family if anyone has any thoughts, comments, or questions. Keep in mind that these are their personal reflections. Considering this, try not to say things like, "No. That is not what the Gospel is saying." Or, "Do you really believe that?" The key is to invite discussion and allow the Lord to lead your family to truthful, inspiring conclusions. Sometimes a child will offer a challenging question or comment. This is good in that it can inspire a healthy search for God and His truth. After everyone has commented, you can add your thoughts, and perhaps suggest a call to action. For example: "Let's make a commitment to pray for the dead." Or, "Let's strive to go out of

our way to do kind acts for one another." 6) Each person can then offer their own prayer intentions. 7) End with thanksgiving to God for His Word and pray a Glory Be.

21. FAMILY PRAYER TIME

The family who prays together stays together (Fr. Patrick Peyton). And even more importantly, a family that prays together stays with God. The key to raising a holy family is being committed to daily family prayer time. Many of your personal methods of praying can be used during family prayer time. For example, the family can pray a couple decades of a scriptural Rosary, Sunday Gospel reflection, Vespers (evening prayer) from the Liturgy of the Hours, reading of Scripture etc. The secret to family prayer is simply doing it. As the father, you have incredible influence on your family. If you lead, most of the time your family will follow. Lead your family to Jesus and Jesus will lead your family. Action steps for implementing and maintaining family prayer include: 1) Establishing a time each evening for family prayer time. 2) Don't make it long—this can make family prayer time a drudgery, especially if the children sense that they are not able to complete homework or have free time. 3) Be consistent, press on, and don't give up. 4) Don't be a drill sergeant and criticize your children for their posture or their lack of attentiveness. 5) Make your prayer personal. Teach your children to pray from their heart. One way to accomplish this is to ask them to voice their petitions. Whether you use the Liturgy of the Hours, Sacred Scripture, or a reflection from a devotional, end your family prayer time with personal prayers of thanksgiving, petition, and praise.

22. FAMILY EVENING TIME

If a modern man was to calculate, at the end of his life, the amount of hours spent at work and then compare them to the amount of hours spent with his family, he would discover that he spent nearly two thirds of his waking hours working and approximately less than a sixth of his waking hours with his family. Considering this, and the fact that we only have— on average—eighteen years of a child living at home with us, our time spent with our children is fleeting and precious. One way to reclaim time with our family for the purpose of fostering strong relationships with them is by making the hours between dinner and bedtime exclusively dedicated to the family. To do this effectively, strive to shut off the television and social media; shut off mobile devices, including your phone unless you need to be on call; and identify activities for the whole family. After dinner is done, and the dishes and kitchen have been cleaned, and after subtracting family prayer time, there is a small chunk of time to spend with your family. This time together is a great tool in solidifying your family and protecting them from the enemy. Too often, children will venture off to their own rooms with their own personal mobile devices and be swept away in virtual worlds that distance them from God and the Church. Your time together as a family is a great aid in overcoming this divisional tactic.

23. BIWEEKLY SON MAN-DATE / DAUGHTER DATE

Children crave individual attention from their parents and in particular from their father. In times past, families and family life were more agrarian; and therefore the family, by its very nature, demanded that children spend more time with their fathers. In the modern age, due to technological advances, particularly in the realm of travel, children receive less individual time and attention from their fathers. By establishing a biweekly man-date with your son or daughter-date with your daughter, you reestablish a connection between you and your child. This commitment to your child communicates that he or she is important to you—important enough for you to sacrifice your own agendas and initiatives for them. The dates need not be anything elaborate;

simply going out for breakfast or coffee is good. The main objective of this time spent with your child is to solidify your relationship; listen and let the child know you care and have an interest in his or her life, express God the Father's generosity (through food and time) and love (attention and listening). Don't have an agenda—meaning, don't take your child out and then drop a bomb about how you are disappointed in them, or have a problem with them that needs resolving. If this occurs, your child will not trust you or want to spend time with you. This demands that the date is a safe zone in which no discipline occurs, and no harsh criticism is made. One key to making this effective is selecting a consistent day and time when the date will occur. If you choose every other Friday, make this a priority and don't break your promise. If a father consistently breaks the "promise" of the daughter-date or man-date, he will break his child's heart. Your greatest treasures are you wife and children. The best money and time you will ever spend is on them.

24. ONE DAILY INTENTIONAL ACT OF ENCOURAGEMENT OR AFFECTION TO YOUR CHILD

A child in today's culture is continually measuring himself against the world's impossible standards. Peer culture and persuasive and pervasive media messages can convince a child to find value and worth in the world, and in the world's evaluation of them. If and when this happens, a child's value will shift based on how they are received by their peers. It is vital that your child knows and understands that their worth and personal value does not shift based on being accepted by peers. To offset and overcome this mentality, it is vital that your child knows that he or she is chosen and not just accepted. To be accepted means that the child is welcome to live with you, use your house and possessions, etc. To let them feel chosen is to intentionally reach out to the child with a hug, a kiss, a blessing, a word of encouragement, or sitting down next to them with the intention to converse with them. The more a child senses that they are valued because of who they are, the more they will believe in God, who loves them for who they are. You can help provide your child with this sense of value by telling your child that you are proud of her; that you love him; that you noticed that he did X, Y, Z and commend him for it. A father's words have prophetic power: speak hope and personal value into them and they will become people of hope who understand their God-given value. Yet, this is a two-edged sword: if you bite at, demean, discourage, and criticize your child, it will no doubt have negative consequences on their ability to perceive themselves as a gift from God. Action steps that can help you in affirming and encouraging your child include identifying things about your child that are of God, and from God; verbally acknowledging those gifts, talents, and abilities; intentionally telling your child that you love him or her; and being physically affectionate with hugs and kisses, roughhousing, etc.

25. INSTALL INTERNET FILTRATION SOFTWARE

No longer does one need to look for immoral, illicit, pornographic content. No. It is looking for us... and our children. Even websites and apps that appear to be safe and secure can often be compromised by links and ads that eventually lead to an immoral trap. The porn industry has spent an enormous amount of money and time devising strategies to have children encounter pornography at an early age for the purpose of engendering a life-long addiction. This life-long addiction means financial growth and stability for those who produce pornography. It has been said that fifteen seconds on the internet can destroy fifteen years of parenting. As protector of your family, it is important to avoid the all-too-common belief: "Not my child." We must understand that it is not your child who is evil, warped, and perverted; but it is your child who can become a victim of such evils. Considering this, it is important to research and determine which internet filtration software is most effective and then purchase and install it.

26. Bless Your Child Daily

You as the human father are a link between heaven and earth, between God and your child. You are called to be the face of the Father that your child cannot see; the voice of the Father that your child cannot hear; and the touch of the Father that your child cannot feel. In the moment of blessing your child, you become the face, the voice, and the touch of the heavenly Father to your child. The fatherly blessing is very powerful, and inculcates a deep love, respect, and trust in your children—trust in you and your fatherhood; and trust in God and His Fatherhood. As with blessing your wife, initially you will experience a feeling of awkwardness and vulnerability, but over time this practice becomes a very loving and natural way to express your love for your child. The keys to blessing your child are selecting a consistent time to bless your child (for many fathers this is prior to bedtime); tracing the sign of the cross over your child's forehead; invoking God's favor and blessing upon your child, and for the grace of restful sleep (if it is prior to bedtime). Hug and embrace your child after the blessing. It may be beneficial to develop your own personal blessing. Regardless, consistency and calling down God the Father's blessing in Christ Jesus' name, and your face, voice, and touch are the key components of this grace-filled practice.

27. One Holy Hour a Week

Once per week, make a visit to a chapel that has Eucharistic Adoration. If you cannot find such a chapel, make it a point to locate a local parish and spend time before our Lord's Eucharistic presence in the tabernacle. Unfortunately, in modern times, Catholic churches are locked, and for good reasons. Yet we must make every effort to either contact the pastor of a parish, obtain a key, or request entrance to the church for a time of prayer. There is nearly nothing as life-changing and transforming as spending time with Christ in Adoration. You cannot give what you do not possess. To give God you must have God; and to have God you must spend time with God; and one of the most powerful ways to spend time with God is in Eucharistic Adoration. By adoring the Lord in His littleness, silence, and hiddenness, you will be given the power to rejoice and be effective in the little, silent, hidden character of your fatherhood. God cannot be outdone in His generosity. Ultimately, it would be ideal to visit our Lord in the Most Blessed Sacrament daily. Regardless, by giving an hour to our Lord once per week, He will grant you incalculable blessings.

28. FREQUENT SACRAMENTS: TAKE CHILD TO ONE DAILY MASS A WEEK/ MONTHLY CONFESSION

One way to convince your child to go to a daily morning Mass is to go out for breakfast/coffee afterward. This connects the two experiences of Mass and Dad-time together. As the child ages, they will associate Holy Mass with a feeling of goodness, warmth, and love, because of the time you spent with them. This connects your love as a father with the love of the heavenly Father. Daily Mass also allows your child to have a more personal connection with the Mass and with Jesus in the Eucharist. Often, Sunday Mass can be distracting and overwhelming. Daily Mass, with its character of silence, affords a more personal experience of Christ, His Word, and His Most Holy Sacrament. Additionally, take your child, and yourself, to the Sacrament of Confession at least once a month. A father who admits that he is a sinner and seeks God's forgiveness sets the standard for his child.

Sometimes we need to "go there," to a place of pilgrimage, to find God "in here," in our hearts. God commanded Moses to erect a "tent of meeting," outside the camp, where Israelites could go to meet with God and receive His guidance. Often, we wonder why our prayer time is compromised, distracted, or ineffective. One of the reasons is that we are praying in an environment that is anything but prayer-ful. When we look around during prayer, we often see paperwork that needs completed, projects that need finishing, dishes that need washing, garbage that needs taking out. The mess of life tends to creep in, making a mess in our soul. A way to battle against this, and even overcome this disadvantage, is by allocating and dedicating a place in your home that is reserved exclusively for prayer. This could be a closet, a basement, or a spare bedroom. Regardless, identify that space and then claim it for the Lord by hanging sacred images there. Use a table as an altar and set your Bible on it; use candles and incense; place statues of Our Lord, our Blessed Mother, and St. Joseph as reminders of your heavenly family. By dedicating a space in your home exclusively to God, you can more effectively dedicate yourself exclusively to God. Additionally, your family will come to understand that God is not an afterthought but the primary reason for your existence.

30. CELEBRATE FEAST DAYS / ABIDE FAST DAYS

A good father connects his domestic church with the liturgical calendar of Holy Mother Church. Therefore, on days of fasting, he guides his family to fast and pray in a way that honors the Lord, without grumbling or complaining. On solemnities and special feast days, especially those related to our Lord Jesus, His Blessed Mother, St. Joseph, and holy patron saints—after whom our children are named—we should strive to be festive, with feasting, desserts, music, singing hymns, and celebrating with family and friends. Another good practice is to honor St. Joseph every Wednesday. By doing so, we create a true liturgical Catholic culture in our domestic church, and our families become connected with the life of Christ as expressed by His Church. One way to make patron saints' feasts more meaningful is to take the child out on a special date. Birthdays and/or baptism days of individual members of the family should also be highly festive and celebrated. Rather than religion being understood as an imposition and a burden, by celebrating such special days we emphasize the joy and generosity of God, and such joy is winsome.

31. Make Sunday Holy

The third commandment is not "Do not work on Sunday," but rather to "Keep holy the Sabbath (the Lord's Day)." Too often, we use Sunday as the day of the week to catch up with duties and chores, or to get ahead by working overtime. Yet God calls us to make Sunday holy by setting it aside for him. The Day of the Lord should be celebratory, familial, expressing to God gratitude and joy for His presence and for the gifts in our lives. We ought to sacrifice our own personal pursuits (see Isaiah 58:13) on Sunday for the Lord who sacrificed himself for us. Ways to make the Lord's Day a day of holiness include: going to Mass on Sunday; having a big breakfast with the family afterward; inviting friends and family over for Sunday dinner; doing something fun as a family; and turning off the television, streaming content, and social media. Don't go shopping or out to restaurants. And offer prayers of thanksgiving before dinner with family and friends. Our culture has made Sunday another day of labor, or a way to increase the value of your home. Reclaim it for the Lord and for your family by setting it aside for God, and God will not be outdone in generosity.

Whether it is doing the dishes after dinner, Saturday housecleaning; landscaping or building retaining walls, remodeling the house, doing plumbing or electrical work, mowing the lawn; sweeping the floor; or changing the little one's diapers, the father should set the pace of self-giving love, that is, initiate an act of service for his family. This simply means that he alerts everyone to the task and then works alongside his children in fulfilling the chore at hand. With joy, and a mind for excellence, he encourages his children to do everything with excellence—not for a wage, but rather at the service of the family. The family is to be like the Trinity: three self-giving persons who are one. We only discover ourselves by giving ourselves away. Familial work is a tremendous gift in that it teaches parents and children to be gifts to one another for the greater good; and in doing this work, everyone discovers personal potential and the joy of serving others. By being involved in familial work, your children come to respect you. Too often a father will leave household chores to his wife and children and venture off to his own hobbies. This type of leadership inculcates disdain and resentment not only for the work, but also for the father. Jesus and Joseph crafted the cross of self-donation in the workshop in Nazareth. Let us, as fathers, learn from them.

33. Sanctify Your Work

"In whatever you do, do it from the heart, as to the Lord, not to men" (Col 3:23). Work is a substantial part of a man's life. Not only does he spend much of his life laboring for a wage, but work is an outlet for creativity and charity, in which man can discover meaning and experience personal fulfillment. Work can also be a massive burden, and extremely dissatisfying. Whether work is fulfilling, or dissatisfying, it can be redeemed by God, by offering it to Christ in union with His salvific work. A father can make his work meaningful, ultimately, by first doing his best to labor with excellence as though he is working for God. Second, he is to offer his work for the redemption of his wife and children, asking God to lavishly grant graces to his family. Yet a father must always bear in mind that his occupation is at the service of his vocation. Therefore his work should not eclipse the primary duties of his vocation, such as family prayer, his own prayer life, family dinner, and the like. There may be circumstances regarding his work that are beyond a father's control, and yet he should do all that he can to place work at the service of his family, rather than his family at the service of his work.

The 33 Practices

Prayer Promises

Morning Offering

Morning Prayer (15 minutes)

Litany to St. Joseph

Rosary / Consecration Prayer to Mary

Family Prayer Daily

Evening Prayer (15 minutes)

Pray with Wife Daily

Daily Examination of Conscience

Pray for Each Member of Your Family

1x To Do's

Establish Tent of Meeting

Sacred Images in Home

Install Internet Filtration

Personal Promises

Be Faithful to Wedding Vows / Be Pure

Abstain from All Work on Sunday

Initiate Serving / Work alongside Children

Avoid Grumbling and Complaining

Daily Commitments

Complete All Prayer Promises Daily

One Hidden Sacrifice

Reduce Use of Radio /Noise and Listen to God

One Intentional Act of Encouragement /Affection to Wife

One Intentional Act of Encouragement /Affection to Children

Bless Your Wife and Children Daily

Give Your Wife 10 Minutes of Intentional Time /Focus on Her

Nightly Family Dinner

Family Evening Time

To Schedule

Weekly /Biweekly Date Night

Son Man-date /Daughter-Date Biweekly

One Holy Hour Minimum Weekly

Take Child Daily Mass Once a Week

Take Child Confession Once a Month

Make Feast Days /Saints' Days Celebratory

Tithe Regularly

Family Gospel Reflection Weekly

Suggested Spiritual Practices Plan

Implementing a rule of life consisting of multiple spiritual practices can be overwhelming. Much like physical training, or education, it is imperative to begin slowly and with the basics; and over time increase the amount of spiritual practices necessary to build your own rule of life. For this reason, The Fathers of St. Joseph suggest the gradual implementation of the spiritual practices over the course of 7 weeks (49 days). Each week select one or two practices that you desire to incorporate into your life. By the end of seven weeks you will have developed your own rule of life. This seven weeks of prayer and penance are a preparation for a new Pentecost, an outpouring of the Holy Spirit on your vocation as husband, father, and head of your household.

WEEK 1 | *Commit to Daily Prayer Practices*

1. Daily Morning Offering
2. Daily Litany of St. Joseph
3. Daily Examination of Conscience
4. Pray for Each Member of Your Family
5. Daily Morning Prayer (15 minutes, including 5 minutes of silence)
6. Daily Rosary
7. Evening Prayer

WEEK 2 | *Commit to Secret Sacrifice*

8. One Daily Hidden Significant Sacrifice
9. Reduce Use of Media Such as Radio, Music, News
10. Avoid Grumbling About or Demeaning Family Members
11. Tithe Regularly / Give to the Poor

WEEK 3 | *Embrace Your Wife*

12. Weekly / Biweekly Date with Your Wife
13. One Daily Intentional Act of Encouragement / Affection to Your Wife
14. Be Faithful to Your Wedding Vows
15. Pray with Your Wife Once a Day
16. Bless Your Wife Daily
17. 10 Minutes of Daily Intentional Time with Your Wife

WEEK 4 | *Build the Domestic Church*

18. Nightly Family Dinner
19. Sacred Images
20. Sunday Gospel Reflection
21. Family Prayer Time
22. Family Evening Time

WEEK 5 | *Embrace Your Child*

23. Biweekly Son Man-date /Daughter-Date
24. One Daily Intentional Act of Encouragement or Affection to Your Child
25. Install Internet Filtration Software
26. Bless Your Child Daily

WEEK 6 | *Live the Liturgical Life*

27. One Holy Hour a Week
28. Frequent Sacraments: Take Child to One Daily Mass a Week and Monthly Confession
29. Establish Your Tent of Meeting
30. Celebrate Feast Days /Abide by Fast Days

WEEK 7 | *Work for God*

31. Abstain from All Work on Sunday
32. Initiate and Be Involved in Family Work
33. Sanctify Your Work

Prayers

Litany to St. Joseph

Lord, have mercy.
Christ, have mercy.
Lord, have mercy.
Christ, hear us.
Christ, graciously hear us.
God, the Father of Heaven, *have mercy on us.*
God the Son, Redeemer of the world, *have mercy on us.*
God the Holy Spirit, *have mercy on us.*
Holy Trinity, One God, *have mercy on us.*
Holy Mary, *pray for us* (after each line)
Saint Joseph,
Renowned offspring of David,
Light of Patriarchs,
Spouse of the Mother of God,
Chaste guardian of the Virgin,
Foster-father of the Son of God,
Diligent protector of Christ,

Head of the Holy Family,
Joseph most just,
Joseph most chaste,
Joseph most prudent,
Joseph most strong,
Joseph most obedient,
Joseph most faithful,
Mirror of patience,
Lover of poverty,
Model of artisans,
Glory of home life,
Guardian of virgins,
Pillar of families,
Solace of the wretched,
Hope of the sick,
Patron of the dying,
Terror of demons,
Protector of Holy Church,
Exemplar of all fathers,

Lamb of God, who takes away the sins of the world,
Spare us, O Lord.
Lamb of God, who takes away the sins of the world,
Graciously hear us, O Lord.
Lamb of God, who takes away the sins of the world,
Have mercy on us.
V. He made him the lord of His house:
R. *And ruler of all His substance.*

Let us pray.

O God, who in Thine unspeakable providence didst vouchsafe to choose blessed Joseph to be the spouse of Thine own most holy Mother; and to be a father to you, O Son of God: grant, we beseech Thee, that we may deserve to have him for our intercessor in heaven, whom we reverence as our defender on earth: who livest and reignest world without end. Amen.

Prayer to Mary and Joseph: O Most Holy Blessed Virgin Mary, St. Joseph her most chaste spouse, my parents in the order of grace, I surrender myself to you. By your holy intercession consecrate me to our Lord Jesus that He may form me ever more fully into a son of God our Father. Amen.

Short Form prayer to Mary and Joseph: Holy Mary, Good St. Joseph, by the power of the Holy Spirit, may I be formed into another Christ. Amen.

Short Form Consecration to Our Lady: Mother I am yours, now and forever, through you and with you, I want to belong, always and only to Jesus.

Prayer to St. Joseph: St. Joseph, gentle and generous, make my heart like yours: little, silent and hidden.

Consecration Prayer to St. Joseph

O St. Joseph predestined and chosen by God from among men, you received the glorious honor of being the chaste, guardian of the Most Blessed Virgin Mary. Inflamed with divine love you received her as your beloved wife and through her God bestowed upon you the most privileged distinction of being the virginal father of God the Son.

As a living reflection of the Heavenly Father, you protected the Christ child from Herod, thus becoming the savior of the Savior. You accepted Jesus' humble submission to your fatherly authority and thus became the master of the Master. As a hidden king you conferred upon Jesus the Davidic kingship and thus became the king of the King of Kings. With untiring joy you labored to nurture the human soul and flesh of Jesus giving bread to the Bread of Life.

Most gentle and generous father, look upon this, your indigent child, and see that I too need your care and protection. O chaste heart that burned with love for Jesus and Mary teach me, your humble servant, to be devoted entirely to Mary and to worship the Lord Jesus with my entire being that I too may become a living reflection of God our Father.

O master of the interior life, you faithfully and promptly fulfilled the divine commands. Your humble obedience has elevated the vocation of fatherhood as a certain means to sublime sanctity and eternal glory. Desiring to follow your holy example, I embrace my vocation to be a most chaste husband, a living icon of God the Father, and a just guardian and guide that my family may become like yours, a holy family.

Therefore, most glorious and humble spiritual father, today before the heavenly host, I surrender myself, my marriage, my fatherhood, my family, my labors, my merits, all that I am and have, unreservedly and totally to you, and consequently to Mary my Queen and most holy Mother, that you may always be my parents in the order of grace and that I may forever be your son. As you and Mary consecrated the Son of God to God the Father, consecrate me also, that I may be set apart for holy service to God most high. I beseech you, as you prepared Christ for His ultimate sacrifice, prepare me also that I may attain the fullness of divine sonship.

Most humble, silent, and hidden father, I surrender all to you that my fatherhood may glorify God the Father of glory in this age and the age to come, forever without end, Amen.

Prayer to St. Joseph

O Saint Joseph, whose protection is so great, so strong, so prompt before the throne of God, I place in you all my interests and desires.

O Saint Joseph, do assist me by your powerful intercession, and obtain for me from your Divine Son all spiritual blessings, through Jesus Christ, our Lord, so that, having engaged here below your heavenly power, I may offer my thanksgiving and homage to the most loving of Fathers.

O Saint Joseph, I never weary contemplating you and Jesus asleep in your arms; I dare not approach while He reposes near your heart. Press Him in my name and kiss his fine head for me and ask Him to return the kiss when I draw my dying breath.

Saint Joseph, patron of departed souls—pray for me. (Mention your intention). Amen.

The above prayer was found in the fiftieth year of our Lord and Savior Jesus Christ. In 1505 it was sent from the pope to Emperor Charles, when he was going into battle. Whoever shall read this prayer or hear it, or keep it about themselves, shall never die a sudden death or be drowned, nor shall poison take effect on them; neither shall they fall into the hands of the enemy, or shall be burned in any fire or shall be overpowered in any battle. Say for nine mornings in a row for anything you may desire. It has never been known to fail.

Consecration Prayer to St. Joseph
by St. Bernadine of Siena

O my beloved Saint Joseph, adopt me as thy child. Take charge of my salvation; watch over me day and night; preserve me from occasions of sin; obtain for me purity of body. Through thy intercession with Jesus, grant me a spirit of sacrifice, humility, self-denial, burning love of Jesus in the Blessed Sacrament, and a sweet and tender love for Mary, my mother. Saint Joseph, be with me living, be with me dying, and obtain for me a favorable judgment from Jesus, my merciful Savior. Amen.

Prayer of St. Francis de Sales

Glorious St. Joseph, Spouse of Mary, grant us, we beseech thee, thy paternal protection, through the Heart of Jesus Christ. O Thou whose infinite power reaches out to all our needs, rendering possible for us that which is impossible, look upon the concerns of thy children with fatherly countenance. In the troubles and sorrows that afflict us, we have confident recourse to thee. Deign to take under thy loving protection this important and difficult endeavor, the cause of our worries, and dispose its success to the glory of God and to the benefit of His faithful servants. Amen.

Spiritual Strategies

To assist you in the spiritual battle we have included several inspired reflections that have aided men in their pursuit to become a holy man of God. We believe that information leads to inspiration, and inspiration leads to transformation, and transformation results in congregation: the assembly of the faithful. May the following excerpts aid you in your pursuit to be the priest of your domestic church.

The Seven R's of Prayer

There is a way to transform our prayer from a monologue to a dialogue; from a relationship to a "real-ationship;" from being filled with words to making us capable of discerning and receiving the true Word. This way is the seven Rs of prayer. The seven Rs is an outline for prayer that if used daily will open you to God who will transform you into a father of glory.

❶ *Recognize God's Presence*

The steps to effective prayer are, first, *recognize* God's presence *in you*. Often we begin prayer, launching into what we want to say, directing our thoughts to the God who seems to be somewhere "out there." Pause and greet God who lives within you. This can be done by making the sign of the cross devoutly and slowly, bowing your head, or simply saying, "Hello, God, I'm here. Hello, God, you are here." But most importantly, we ought to pause for a moment of silence reverently acknowledging that we are humbly placing ourselves in the presence of God who has placed His presence within us.

❷ Read God's Word

Second, every conversation has a context, a topic for discussion. It is no different with our relationship with God. Considering this, the second R of prayer is *read*. It is important to read God's Word, particularly the Gospel, which contextualizes our prayer. We read until something strikes us, or a phrase connects with us. Perhaps we reread the same passage a couple of times.

❸ Reflect on a Word or Phrase

Third, after you have identified a phrase or a word that God is using to speak to you, *reflect* on that word or phrase. Meditate and consider what God is trying to communicate to you through His word.

❹ Respond to God

Fourth, after reflecting, we *respond* to God. We do this by discussing our dreams, aspirations, desires, struggles, plans for the day, our sins, fears, and anxieties—we simply tell Him all about it. During this time we ask for His help and guidance, and for Him to grant success to the work of our hands (see Psalm 90).

❺ Rest in God

The fifth R is *rest*. After you have recognized God's presence, read His Word, reflected on the phrase that resonates with you, and responded to His Word, then it is time to rest in Him. Simply remain in His presence silently for several minutes. This, perhaps, is the most essential aspect of prayer. During this time of rest God infuses His very presence and life into us.

6 *Make a Resolution*

Sixth, after you have rested in God, then make a *resolution* in the form of a request: God please help me do this today.

7 *Remember Your Resolution*

The seventh R is to *remember* your resolution throughout the day, returning to the divine guidance that you received during prayer.

By humbly entering the silence daily and listening in this manner, you can be certain that God will transform your life. You will become a father of purpose, peace, power, and passion, who is capable of transmitting God's love and mercy to his family.

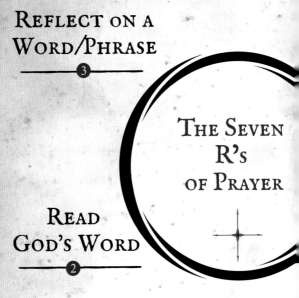

REFLECT ON A
WORD/PHRASE
③

THE SEVEN
R's
OF PRAYER

READ
GOD'S WORD
②

RECOGNIZE
GOD'S PRESENCE
①

RESPOND TO GOD
4

REST IN GOD
5

MAKE A RESOLUTION
6

REMEMBER YOUR RESOLUTION
7

The Devil's
Six Darts

Your fatherly vocation has been divinely designed to enable you to be lifted up (your crucifixion), and by your sacrificial love draw those around you to Christ and His love (your glorification). Your exaltation demands nothing less than a resolute and enduring faith in God. Faith is more than assenting intellectually to a belief or truth. In its deepest essence, faith is trust in another person, ultimately trust in God, and the truth of His identity. Original sin attempts to abolish from our hearts trust in the Father's love "Original sin then attempts to abolish fatherhood"—St. John Paul II).

For this reason, it is vital that "In all things take up the shield of faith, wherewith you may be able to quench all the fiery darts of the most wicked one"

(Eph 6). Again, faith is trust in God, *your* Father, and such trust deflects and extinguishes the fiery darts of the devil and affords you the confidence and freedom to become who you are intended to be: a manifestation and revelation of God's glory. The evil one assails us with six darts for the purpose of preventing us from being lifted up in sacrificial glory.

These six darts are: doubt, discouragement, deprecation, disobedience, despair, and ultimately death.

❶ Doubt (Rooted in Deception)
The dart of doubt (always rooted in a type of deception) instills a mistrust of God and lures us into believing that God is neglecting us; that He is distant; that He is against us; that He will not bless us as He blesses others; and that He is the source of our angst, trials, and sufferings.

❷ Discouragement
When we doubt God and His fatherhood we become discouraged; we lose the courage and will to sacrifice, to battle and suffer for something transcendent and greater—such as the salvation of your wife and children—rather than temporary, illusive fleshly appetites and comforts.

DEPRECATION

3

DISCOURAGEMENT →

2

DOUBT

1

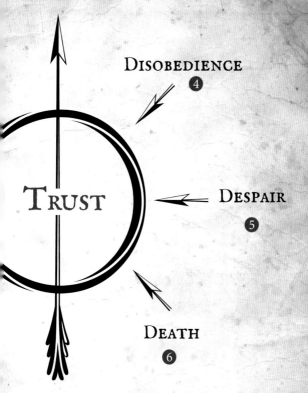

HEAVEN

DISOBEDIENCE
4

TRUST

DESPAIR
5

DEATH
6

YOU & YOUR
FAMILY

❸ Deprecation (Feeling Defeated)

After the disease of discouragement lodges itself into our souls we will be tempted to self-deprecate, that is, to think less of ourselves rather than thinking of ourselves less. Self-deprecation manifests itself in behaviors like self-pity; measuring and comparing ourselves to others; saying things to ourselves about ourselves that are not echoing the voice of God.

❹ Disobedience

Such self-pity can often convince us to lift ourselves from our desperation by attempting to do something that grants us temporary self-worth. This action is usually expressed in an act of disobedience that is contrary to God's will, such as using women to make us feel more like a man, grasping for more because we feel like we are less, pretending to be someone else because we resent the person we are.

❺ Despair

Eventually we wake from our dazed stupor of disobedience and become dejected due to the new awareness of our sins. It is during this moment that the evil one turns on us, rubs our noses in our sinful poop, and attempts to convince us that our sins are unforgivable, for the purpose of leading us into despair.

6 Death

Such despair convinces us to avoid turning to God and instead remain in the depravity of ongoing continual sin. Such despair ultimately leads to the death of the soul.

"Let no man, when he is tempted, say that he is tempted by God. For God is not a tempter of evils, and he tempteth no man; But every man is tempted by his own concupiscence, being drawn away and allured. Then when concupiscence hath conceived, it bringeth forth sin. But sin, when it is completed, begetteth death." (Jas 1:13-16). In other words, the foundation of every sin is mistrust in God's fatherhood instilled by the fiery dart of doubt, which leads to erroneous, misleading desires. But "Blessed is the man who endures trial, for when he stood the test he will receive the crown of life which God has promised to those who love him" (Jas 1:12).

St. Joseph, after discovering his wife, Mary, pregnant without his cooperation, was assailed by doubt. However, Joseph turned to God, changed his course, and reconciled himself to God and Mary. We also will do well to learn from Joseph how to overcome the dart of doubt and turn in trust to God our Father in time of trial.

The Devil's Four Tactics

Your fatherly vocation is the path by which you are to travel from this earth to heaven. It is through your vocation that you will hear the *Vox*, the Word that helps you discover your true identity and thus attain your destiny.

The hellish bully, the evil one, stands amidst this path, tirelessly attempting to intimidate you and drive you from it. He will do nearly anything to keep you from hearing the voice of God, because he knows that if you cannot hear the orders from your divine captain you certainly cannot fulfill them. Indeed, if you cannot hear the Word regarding your identity, you cannot lead your family to their destiny.

The evil one knows that you are called to be a manifestation, a revelation of God's fatherly glory. If the devil drives you from your vocation, the many people to whom you would have revealed God's glory may never encounter Him and be eternally lost. And so would the others that they would have touched down through the decades and centuries.

The evil one's strategy can be described as having four aspects or stages: temptation, intimidation, distraction, and isolation.

❶ *Temptation*

The first stage is temptation. If the evil one cannot tempt you or keep you in mortal or ongoing venial sin, he will use intimidation to drive you from your vocational path. If he cannot intimidate you, he will use the tactic of distraction; and if he cannot distract you from your vocation, he will lure you into isolation.

The essence of this truth is disclosed by Jesus in the Parable of the Sower and the Seed. Jesus interprets the birds that steal the seed sowed on the wayside as the devil who robs us of the seed of the Word, the voice of God, which speaks of our identity, mission, and destiny. The evil one robs us of the seed before it can take root by means of temptation. When a man is bound by such temptations he cannot hear the Word nor is he truly capable of transmitting it to his wife and children.

❷ *Intimidation*

If the devil cannot lead you into temptation, he will try to intimidate you. Jesus said that the seed that fell on rocky soil and was scorched by the sun because it had no roots symbolizes those who initially believe, but when they are persecuted or experience suffering because of their belief in Jesus, lose heart and fall away.

❸ *Distraction*

If the evil one cannot tempt us or intimidate us, he will distract us. Jesus said the seed that began to spring up was choked by thorns and thistles, which symbolize the pursuit of pleasures and riches, and the cares of the world. The evil one derives great pleasure in giving us something good for the purpose of keeping us from that which is greatest. Money, entertainment, relaxation, hobbies, and pleasure are all good, but if they rob your attention from God, your wife, and children, they become an obstacle to the success of your vocation.

❹ *Isolation*

If he cannot lure us with temptation, intimidation, or distraction, the devil will use the tactic of isolation.

Isolation occurs when we separate ourselves from people because we don't believe them to be as holy as we are. By doing this we separate ourselves from God. Hence the name "Pharisee" actually means *separated one*. Isolation also occurs when we separate ourselves from God because we don't believe that we are holy enough, and consequently we separate ourselves from His people.

Consider St. Joseph. When he discovered Mary pregnant without his cooperation, he initially withdrew from his vocational path and decided to separate himself from Mary. The evil one intimidated and tempted Joseph to believe that he was not worthy of Mary—or God within her—attempting to drive him into isolation. Joseph, rather than isolating himself from God, placed himself in prayerful silent solitude *with* God. It was in the silent solitude that Joseph received the *Vox*, the Word, the voice that communicated his identity and mission: "Joseph son of David [this is his identity: he is a son of David and therefore a son of God], do not fear to take Mary your wife, for that which is conceived in her is of the Holy Spirit [this is his vocation: to be a husband to the Mother of God and a father to the Son of God]."

Remain strong like Joseph. Do not give the devil permission to drive you from your vocational path.

By following St. Joseph's heroic example and relying upon his intercession, you can overcome temptation, intimidation, distraction, and isolation. By doing so, you will begin to discover your identification in your vocation will lead your family to their destination, which is their glorification—their deification.

The Power
Behind Prayer

Charity, the greatest of all virtues, is friendship (communion) with God. Being a friend of God and living in communion with God is the greatest thing that you or I will ever do or experience.

There are three foundational components of friendship: trust, communication, and self-donation. By means of communication, combined with self-donation, trust in the other is developed. If I sacrifice for my wife, yet never communicate with her, or if I communicate with my wife, yet never sacrifice for her, our relationship will lack trust and intimacy, never achieving the full expression and stature of love. And so it is with our friendship with God.

In order for our friendship with God to express the full measure of love, it is imperative that we communicate with God, which is prayer, and donate ourselves to God, which is sacrifice. This is where our spiritual location and living our vocation meet; where silence and sacrifice merge; where prayer and action integrate. We've discussed how to pray (communicate with God), but what gives prayer power?

Our Lord, responding to His apostle's question about why they could not exorcise a demon from a young boy, said, "Only by prayer and fasting can this kind be expelled." If our prayer is to be powerful, our prayer must be animated by secret sacrifice. Prayer without sacrifice is lip service, and sacrifice without prayer is the mere submission of the body and the training of one's own will. Secret sacrifice inspires our prayer, and prayer inspires us to sacrifice in secret.

Remember that your vocation is your path to glory. Therefore, it is within your vocation (marriage and fatherhood) that you will discover how to sacrifice truly.

Ite ad Joseph

Your Next Steps

40 DAYS
TO FATHERLY GREATNESS
LEAD FOR INDIVIDUALS

CUSTOS
TOTAL CONSECRATION THROUGH SAINT JOSEPH

LEAD
THE FOUR MARKS OF FATHERLY GREATNESS
MEN'S GROUPS